MAKING A DIFFERENCE: **LEADERS WHO ARE CHANGING THE WORLD**

AUNG SAN SUU KYI

MYANMAR'S FREEDOM FIGHTER

LAURA LA BELLA

Britannica
Educational Publishing

IN ASSOCIATION WITH

ROSEN
EDUCATIONAL SERVICES

Published in 2015 by Britannica Educational Publishing (a trademark of Encyclopædia Britannica, Inc.) in association with The Rosen Publishing Group, Inc.
29 East 21st Street, New York, NY 10010

Distributed exclusively by Rosen Publishing.
To see additional Britannica Educational Publishing titles, go to rosenpublishing.com.

First Edition

Britannica Educational Publishing
J.E. Luebering: Director, Core Reference Group
Anthony L. Green: Editor, Compton's by Britannica

Rosen Publishing
Hope Lourie Killcoyne: Executive Editor
Jeanne Nagle: Editor
Nelson Sá: Art Director
Michael Moy: Designer
Cindy Reiman: Photography Manager
Amy Feinberg: Photo Researcher

Cataloging-in-Publication Data
La Bella, Laura, author.
Aung San Suu Kyi: Myanmar's freedom fighter/Laura La Bella.—First edition.
    pages cm.—(Making a difference: leaders who are changing the world)
Audience: 5–8.
Includes bibliographical references and index.
ISBN 978-1-62275-430-4 (library bound)—ISBN 978-1-62275-432-8 (pbk.)—
ISBN 978-1-62275-433-5 (6-pack)
1. Aung San Suu Kyi—Juvenile literature. 2. Women political activists—Burma—Biography—Juvenile literature. 3. Women political prisoners—Burma—Biography—Juvenile literature. 4. Women Nobel Prize winners—Burma—Biography—Juvenile literature. 5. Democracy—Burma—Juvenile literature. 6. Burma—Politics and government—1988—Juvenile literature. I. Title.
DS530.53.A85L83 2014
959.105092—dc23
[B]

2014004233

Manufactured in the United States of America

CONTENTS

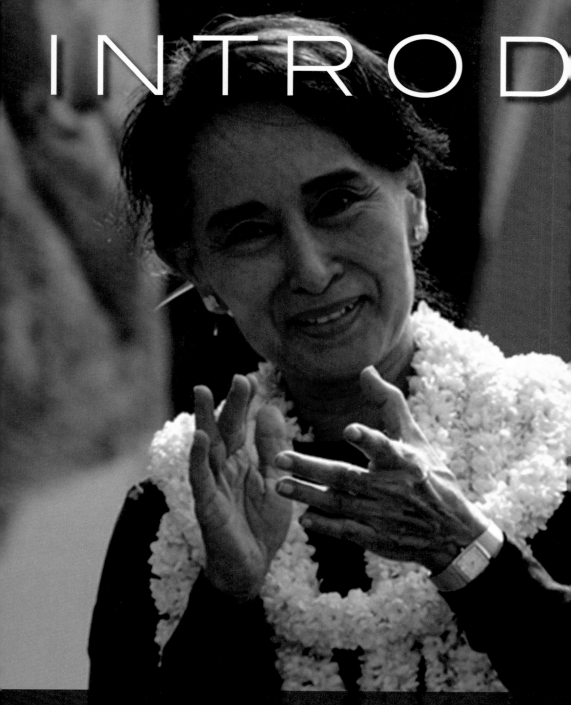

Aung San Suu Kyi has tirelessly fought for independence, democracy, and human rights for the people of Burma. She continues to be a strong, positive force in the country today.

A round the world, Aung San Suu Kyi is known as a fighter for democracy and human rights. In her country of Myanmar (which used to be known as Burma), she has taken on the junta, or military group that took political power. She has spoken out against the way the government is run and how poorly the people have been treated. Three separate times she has been arrested and sentenced to house arrest, unable to leave her home or visit her family. In total, she has spent more than fifteen years under house arrest.

Suu Kyi's tireless efforts to establish a democratic government and ensure freedoms for her people have been recognized around the world. She has received the Nobel Peace Prize and has been the recipient of nearly every major human rights award, including the European Union's Sakharov Prize, the Professor Thorolf Rafto Memorial Prize, the Jawaharlal Nehru Award, and the International Simón Bolívar Prize.

But to her many followers, Suu Kyi is simply known as "the Lady," a woman who has sacrificed her rights in the name of freedom for the people of Myanmar.

Aung San Suu Kyi was born in Rangoon, the former capital of Burma, on June 19, 1945. Since 1989, Burma has been called the Republic of the Union of Myanmar, or Myanmar for short. It is the second-largest country in Southeast Asia and is bordered by China, Thailand, India, Laos, and Bangladesh.

Suu Kyi was the youngest child of Aung San and Khin Kyi. She had two older brothers, Aung San Oo and Aung San Lin. Suu Kyi was only two years old when her father, Aung San, died. A fighter

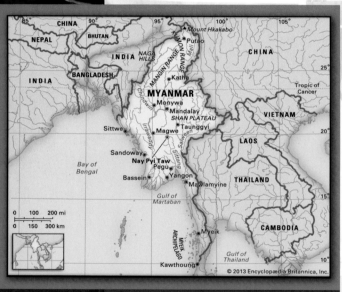

Map of Myanmar.

Two-year-old Suu Kyi *(bottom center)* in 1947 with her parents and two older brothers.

for Burmese freedom from British rule, Aung San was assassinated six months before the country gained its independence in 1948.

Suu Kyi lived in Burma until 1960. She and her brother Aung San Oo—her other brother, Aung San Lin, had drowned in 1953—then traveled to India with their mother, a diplomat

7

QUICK FACT

Although Myanmar is considered the country's official name, many people, especially those who support Aung San Suu Kyi, still refer to the country as Burma. Because the military dictatorship changed the country's name to Myanmar, it remains U.S. policy to refer to the country as Burma in most contexts.

who served as Burma's first female ambassador. From 1960 to 1967, Khin Kyi was the Burmese ambassador to India and Nepal.

EDUCATION AND EARLY CAREER

After graduating from high school, Suu Kyi moved to England and became a student at the University of Oxford. She earned a bachelor of arts degree in philosophy, politics, and economics. Oxford is where she met her future husband, Michael Aris, an expert on Tibetan and Himalayan culture.

Suu Kyi moved to New York City, where she worked for the United Nations. She worked as an assistant secretary for the Advisory Committee on Administrative and Budgetary Questions.

In 1971, Suu Kyi married Aris. They lived in Bhutan for a year, where Suu Kyi worked as a research officer of the Royal Ministry of Foreign

Michael Aris and Suu Kyi outside an office in Kensington, London, where they had registered to be married.

Affairs. In 1973, the couple settled in the city of Oxford to raise their two sons, Alexander, born in 1973, and Kim, born in 1977.

SCHOLARSHIP AND PUBLISHING

Before Suu Kyi became a pro-democracy leader, her career was centered mostly on education and research. After getting married, she served as a visiting scholar at the Center of Southeast Asian Studies at Kyoto University in Japan. It was here that she began to do some research about the time her father had spent in Japan. In 1984, she published *Aung San*, a biography of father. While she

QUICK FACT

In addition to a biography of her father, Aung San Suu Kyi has also published travel books on Nepal, Bhutan, and Burma.

was living in Japan, she also published the article "Socio-Political Currents in Burmese Literature, 1910-1940" in a Tokyo University journal.

Upon her return to England, Suu Kyi enrolled in the London School of Oriental and African Studies with the intent of completing an advanced degree. Her schooling was cut short when her mother became ill and Suu Kyi went back to Burma to care for her.

RETURN TO BURMA

In addition to being a scholar, wife, and mother, Suu Kyi was a dutiful and loving daughter. When her mother (who had returned to Burma after her appointment as ambassador had ended) suffered a stroke, Suu Kyi traveled to care for her. She left her husband and sons behind in England.

During this trip home, Suu Kyi witnessed human rights violations committed by the military junta that had taken control of the country. She saw for herself how poorly the country's people were being treated. Many people were out of work and starving, and the military junta was involved in a civil war along

Suu Kyi speaks to the crowd at a 1989 rally in Burma. She publicly criticized the country's military leadership.

its borders. Civilians who were protesting conditions in the country were being killed in the streets.

Her mother died in 1988, but Suu Kyi decided to stay in Burma. Conditions in her home country upset her. She decided she should follow in her parents' footsteps and become involved in the country's political scene. She began to speak out against the military junta. Doing so helped her to become a symbol of hope for her people.

A LEGACY OF PUBLIC SERVICE

Both of Aung San Suu Kyi's parents served their country. Her father was a leader of the independence movement in the 1940s, and her mother was among the first women to become involved in Burmese politics. Their political and governmental careers were a powerful influence on Suu Kyi's life.

A FATHER'S STRENGTH

Aung San began his fight for Burmese independence shortly after he graduated from Rangoon University in 1938. During World War II, he teamed up with the Japanese, partly because they promised to help Burma break free from British rule. With the help of the Japanese military, he formed the Burmese Independence Army. Unhappy about how his troops were being treated, and afraid that Japan would be on the losing side of the war, he later started working with the Allies, which included Great Britain.

After the war, Aung San became a leading political figure in Burma. The Burmese government was still under British control, however. Aung San worked hard to negotiate Burma's independence from Great

Suu Kyi's father, Aung San, was an important political figure in Burma — and a great influence on his daughter.

Britain. In 1947, working with British prime minister Clement Attlee, he got the British government to agree to grant Burma independence within one year.

There were hopes that Aung San would become prime minister of the newly

QUICK FACT

Aung San Suu Kyi was named after family members, which is a common practice in Asian cultures. In Burmese, her name means "a bright collection of strange victories."

independent nation. That never happened because he was assassinated before Burmese independence could be achieved.

A MOTHER'S EXAMPLE

Khin Kyi served her nation as a member of parliament in the country's first post-independence government, formed after her husband's death. In 1960, she was appointed as Burma's ambassador to India, becoming the country's first woman to serve in

Suu Kyi's mother, Khin Kyi, and her two sons standing in front of a picture of Aung San in 1949, two years after he was killed.

17

such a position. She served as ambassador for six years before returning to her home country.

Khin Kyi died on December 28, 1988, at the age of seventy-six. More than two hundred thousand people attended her funeral, despite a strong military presence put in place to keep the Burmese people from attending.

FOLLOWING HER PARENTS' PATH

At first Suu Kyi did not want anything to do with public life. For the most part, she was content to teach, study, and raise her two sons. In *Voice of Hope*, a book written with journalist Alan Clements, Suu Kyi described how her

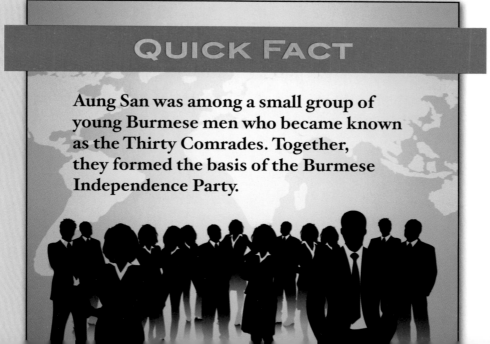

QUICK FACT

Aung San was among a small group of young Burmese men who became known as the Thirty Comrades. Together, they formed the basis of the Burmese Independence Party.

father's difficult past in politics, as well as his assassination, discouraged her from getting involved in efforts toward democracy for Burma. She saw the sacrifices he made, including giving his life for his nation's freedom.

Suu Kyi places flowers on her father's tomb on a day honoring Aung San and other fallen Burmese independence fighters.

After her mother died, however, Suu Kyi had a change of heart. Rather than living in England and staying out of matters in her home country, she felt it was necessary to publicly join the antigovernment movement that had been growing in Burma.

Her first public appearance in support of the country's pro-democracy movement occurred in August 1988, shortly after a mass

Suu Kyi *(center)* speaks at an antimilitary rally in August 1988, which marks her first appearance in support of the country's pro-democracy movement.

killing of protesters. In front of a temple in Rangoon, she spoke about the need for people to band together and fight for democracy. Throughout the speech she talked about her father, what he had stood for, and all the good he had done for the country and its citizens. She also mentioned that what she had seen

QUICK FACT

Freedom from Fear: And Other Writings, a collection of Suu Kyi's articles and speeches edited by her husband, Michael Aris, was published in 1991.

while caring for her sick mother had convinced her that she should enter into the world of politics.

"The present crisis is the concern of the entire nation. I could not, as my father's daughter, remain indifferent to all that was going on," she told the crowd. "This national crisis could in fact be called the second struggle for national independence."

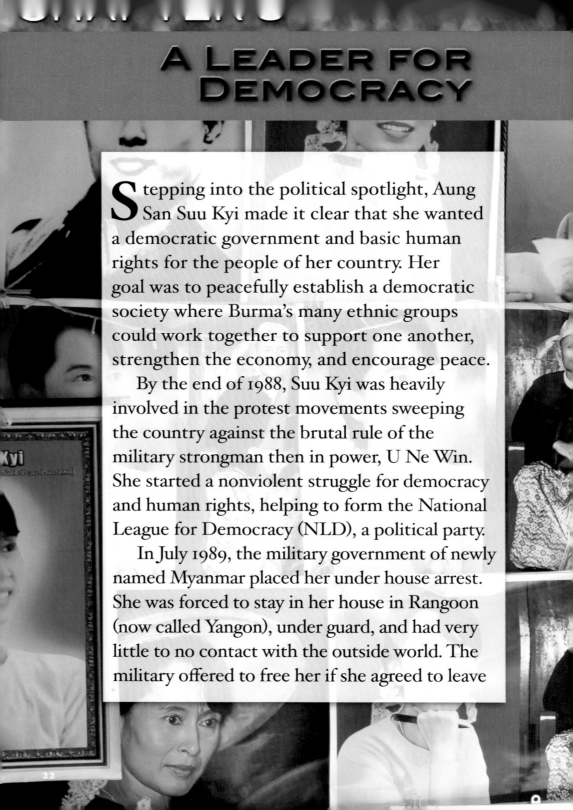

Stepping into the political spotlight, Aung San Suu Kyi made it clear that she wanted a democratic government and basic human rights for the people of her country. Her goal was to peacefully establish a democratic society where Burma's many ethnic groups could work together to support one another, strengthen the economy, and encourage peace.

By the end of 1988, Suu Kyi was heavily involved in the protest movements sweeping the country against the brutal rule of the military strongman then in power, U Ne Win. She started a nonviolent struggle for democracy and human rights, helping to form the National League for Democracy (NLD), a political party.

In July 1989, the military government of newly named Myanmar placed her under house arrest. She was forced to stay in her house in Rangoon (now called Yangon), under guard, and had very little to no contact with the outside world. The military offered to free her if she agreed to leave

At her home in Yangon, Suu Kyi is seen putting her thoughts down on paper while under house arrest. Even while confined, Suu Kyi continued to fight for the Burmese people.

Myanmar, but she refused to do so until the country was returned to civilian government. In the 1990 parliamentary elections, the NLD won more than 80 percent of the seats that were contested. The military government ignored the election results, however, and did not allow the new parliament to meet.

QUICK FACT

Although banned from political activity after her release in 1995, Suu Kyi was, at first, allowed to make speeches every weekend. The junta put a stop to her speeches in 1996.

In 1995, Suu Kyi was freed from house arrest, but she was barred from leading the National League for Democracy. Accused of having broken travel restrictions, she was again placed under house arrest in 2000, but she was released about a year and a half later. Following clashes between the NLD and pro-government demonstrators in 2003, the government returned Suu Kyi to house arrest. The international community issued strong calls for her release.

In May 2009, shortly before her sentence was to be completed, an intruder (a U.S. citizen) entered her house compound and

END MILITARY JUNTA IN

WANTED

FREE BURMA NOW!!!

FREE DAW

Demonstrators in the Philippines protest Suu Kyi's house arrest and the military leadership in Myanmar in 2007.

spent two nights there. Suu Kyi was arrested and convicted of breaching the terms of her house arrest. At first, the court sentenced her to three years of hard labor, but the ruling junta leader at the time, General Than Shwe, reduced the sentence to a year and a half. He also declared that she could serve her time back under house arrest rather than doing hard labor.

It was widely believed that this conviction was intended to prevent her from participating in the 2010 multiparty parliamentary elections—the first to be held since 1990. Indeed, in 2010, new election laws barred individuals who had been convicted of a crime from participating. They also prohibited anyone who was married to a foreign national (as Suu Kyi was) from running for office.

In support of Suu Kyi, the NLD refused to reregister under these new laws, as was required. As a result, the party was disbanded.

QUICK FACT

The National League for Democracy was founded to help establish a multiparty government, support human rights, and return the country to a government that followed the rule of law.

In the November 2010 elections, the
government parties won an overwhelming
majority of legislative seats amid widespread
allegations of voter fraud.

Six days after the elections, Suu Kyi was
released from house arrest. She vowed to
continue her opposition to military rule.

A crowd of supporters celebrate the 2010 release of Suu
Kyi *(center)* outside her home in Yangon.

27

PAYING A HUGE PRICE

Suu Kyi's dedication to Burma has not been without personal sacrifices. While under house arrest, there were long periods of time when she could not even communicate with her husband and children. She has gone long stretches, sometimes up to ten years, without seeing her two sons.

Perhaps the highest price Suu Kyi had to pay came in the late 1990s. Her husband, Michael, was diagnosed with cancer. He was denied a visa to go to Myanmar and be with her while she was under house arrest. Fearful that she would not be allowed back into the country, Suu Kyi did not accept the government's offer for her to travel to England to care for him. That fear also kept her from attending Aris's funeral in 1999.

MAKING THE MOST OF FREEDOM

Government restrictions on Suu Kyi's postrelease activities were relaxed during 2011. She was allowed to meet with Myanmar's new civilian president, Thein Sein. Other

Former U.S. secretary of state Hillary Clinton meets with Suu Kyi in Yangon to discuss democracy in Myanmar.

high-profile meetings followed later in the year, including those with Thailand's new prime minister, Yingluck Shinawatra, in October and U.S. secretary of state Hillary Clinton in December.

Meanwhile, rules on political participation were eased, and the NLD was officially

QUICK FACT

In 2009, a United Nations body declared that Suu Kyi being kept under house arrest was illegal under Myanmar's own law.

reinstated. In January 2012, Suu Kyi announced that she was seeking election to represent the people of Yangon. Her bid to run for office was approved by the government in February. She easily won her seat in the April 1 elections and was sworn into office on May 2.

CHAPTER 4

HONORED FOR HER DEDICATION

S uu Kyi's dedication to her country has endeared her to the Burmese people. It has also won her the respect and admiration of other world leaders, human rights groups, and ordinary people around the globe. Several organizations have chosen to present Suu Kyi with awards that recognize her efforts working toward justice for the Burmese people, as well as a number of other worthy causes.

AWARDED THE NOBEL PEACE PRIZE

In 1991, Suu Kyi was awarded the Nobel Prize for Peace. At the time she was under house arrest and was unable to accept the award in person. In her place, her husband and sons, Alexander and Kim, traveled to Oslo, Norway, to accept the award in her place. Suu Kyi announced that she would use the $1.3 million prize money to establish a health and education trust for the Burmese people.

The Myanmar government responded to the news that Suu Kyi was being given the Nobel Peace Prize by telling stories and spreading rumors that made her look bad.

In 2012, Suu Kyi traveled outside Myanmar for the first time since 1988. During a tour of Europe, she was finally able to give her acceptance speech for the Nobel Prize in Oslo. During her Nobel Lecture on June 16 of that year, she mentioned that being under house arrest made her feel unreal. "There was the house which was my world, there was the world of others who also were not free but who were together in prison as a community, and there was the world of the free," she said.

Suu Kyi in Oslo, Norway, delivers her acceptance speech twenty-one years after winning the Nobel Prize for Peace.

"Each was a different planet pursuing its own separate course in an indifferent universe."

She credited receiving the Nobel Prize with making her feel as if she was a part of the "human community" again, not separated from anyone in any way. "And what was more important," she said, "the Nobel Prize had drawn the attention of the world to the struggle for democracy and human rights in Burma. We were not going to be forgotten."

OTHER AWARDS AND HONORS

Before winning the Nobel Peace Prize, Suu Kyi had the honor of receiving the Thorolf Rafto Memorial Prize. Named for a Norwegian peace

QUICK FACT

In 2011, a film titled *The Lady* hit theaters. Starring Michelle Yeoh, the film chronicles the life of Aung San Suu Kyi, her marriage to Michael Aris, and her dedication to the people of Burma as she fights for democracy.

and human rights activist, the Rafto Prize is given each year to someone who has staged an outstanding fight for freedom and democracy. The Rafto Foundation committee awarded her the prize "for her peaceful struggle under the military dictatorship."

Also in 1990, Suu Kyi was awarded the Sakharov Prize for Freedom of Thought,

Suu Kyi receives the Sakharov Prize in 2013. Over the years, several human rights groups have honored Suu Kyi for her work toward a free and democratic Myanmar.

EUROPEAN PARLIAMENT

35

SAKHAROV PRIZE 1990
FOR FREEDOM OF THOUGHT
AWARDED TO
NG SAN SUU KYI

presented to her by the European Parliment. The prize is named after Andrei Sakharov, a scientist in the former Soviet Union who fought for civil liberties in his country.

Suu Kyi has received other similar prizes over the years. In 1992, she was named the winner of the International Simón Bolívar Prize. This award is given to individuals for outstanding work toward achieving freedom and justice. The Jawaharlal Nehru Award for International Understanding, presented to Suu Kyi in 1993, is named in honor of the former prime minister of India. Nehru was a crusader for peace and international harmony.

QUICK FACT

During her house arrest, Suu Kyi posted a quote from the writings of Indian leader Jawaharlal Nehru that read, in part, "Any achievement that is based on widespread fear can hardly be a desirable one."

The United States has recognized Suu Kyi's work by awarding her the nation's two most important civilian honors. In 2000, President Bill Clinton awarded her the Presidential Medal of Freedom. This award is given to those who have done exceptional work toward, among other things, world peace. In 2007, the U.S. House of Representatives voted unanimously to give Suu Kyi the Congressional Gold Medal. She was the first person ever to receive the award while imprisoned or under house arrest.

In addition to these awards, Suu Kyi has also received honorary degrees from a number of colleges and universities around the world.

UNITED NATIONS GLOBAL ADVOCATE

In 2012, Suu Kyi was invited to serve as a Global Advocate for Zero Discrimination with the Joint United Nations Programme on HIV/ AIDS. UNAIDS, as the program is known, strives to fight discrimination against those affected by AIDS and HIV. In a news release announcing her new role, Suu Kyi said, "It is a

Suu Kyi speaks on behalf of AIDS patients everywhere. She is shown here with Michel Sidibe on World AIDS Day in 2014.

great honour to be chosen as a champion for people who live on the fringes of society and struggle every day to maintain their dignity and basic human rights. I would like to be the voice of the voiceless."

Working Toward Constitutional Reform

In November 2013, Suu Kyi spoke at the Sydney Opera House in Sydney, Australia. She spoke of her commitment to establishing democracy in her country and the need for human rights. She also talked about the need to make changes to the country's constitution.

Many people believe that Suu Kyi was hoping to change the constitution so that she could run for president of Myanmar in 2015. Before the 2010 national elections, the Myanmar government added clauses to the constitution that prevent certain people— her in particular—from running for such a high office.

A group of parliament members collected proposed amendments, or changes, to the junta-written constitution. Written by lawmakers and even the general public, the proposals were submitted in early 2014 so that members of Myanmar's parliament could consider making them law.

STILL FIGHTING THE GOOD FIGHT

Aung San Suu Kyi traveled around Myanmar to gain support for the constitution reform movement. Even though the junta was supposedly no longer in power after 2011, the military was still very much involved in the

"The Lady" continues to travel around the world to raise awareness of the fight for democracy in her home country. Here, she waves to supporters after returning from Europe.

country's politics. In January 2014, the military refused to let a plane carrying Suu Kyi land at an airport near where she was supposed to give a speech about changing the constitution because it was a military airport. She was also barred from using a nearby field for a rally at which she would speak.

Suu Kyi did not let this interruption keep her from completing her speaking tour. Her plane landed at a civilian airport, and she took a car to the city that was the next stop on her tour. As she had shown during years of house arrest and other means the junta had taken to keep her out of the public eye, Suu Kyi would not be silenced. She would continue to fight for the rights of her people as the strong leader she has proven to be.

1964: Studies at Oxford University.

1969–1971: Works at United Nations.

1984: Publishes *Aung San*, a biography of her father.

1985–1986: Visiting scholar at the Center for Southeast Asian Studies, Kyoto University, Japan.

April 1988: Returns to Burma.

August 1988: Makes first public speech; calls for a multiparty democratic government.

September 1988: Establishes the National League for Democracy (NLD); becomes general-secretary.

July 1989: First placed under house arrest.

May 1990: NLD wins big in legislative election; military junta won't recognize results.

1990: Awarded Professor Thorolf Rafto Memorial Prize; awarded Sakharov Prize for Freedom of Thought.

October 1991: Awarded Nobel Peace Prize.

1992: Awarded the International Simón Bolívar Prize.

1993: Awarded the Jawaharlal Nehru Award.

1995: Released from house arrest; military limits political involvement.

September 2000: Placed under house arrest for second time.

December 2000: Awarded Presidential Medal of Freedom by U.S. president Bill Clinton.

May 2002: Released from house arrest.

May 2003: Placed under third house arrest.

2008: Awarded the Congressional Gold Medal by U.S. president George W. Bush.

May 2009: Arrested and charged with violating the terms of her house arrest when an American visits her home uninvited.

August 2009: Found guilty of violating house arrest; sentenced to eighteen additional months.

November 2010: Released from her third house arrest.

December 2011: NLD permitted to register for future elections.

April 2012: Wins a seat in parliament in first multiparty elections since 1990.

May 2012: Travels outside of Burma for the first time since 1988; visits Bangkok, Thailand.

June 1, 2012: Speaks at World Economic Forum on East Asia.

June 16, 2012: Delivers acceptance speech for Nobel Peace Prize in Oslo, Norway.

June 21, 2012: Addresses both houses of the British Parliament.

November 2013: Delivers speech at event in Sydney, Australia, where she expresses a desire to become president of Myanmar.

- **César Chávez.** This Mexican American farmworker dedicated his life to improving the treatment, pay, and working conditions of farm workers. He formed the National Farm Workers Association, which later became United Farm Workers.

- **Bill and Hillary Clinton.** The former U.S. president and his wife, former U.S. secretary of state, are the founders of the Clinton Global Initiative, which unites world leaders to create and implement solutions to some of the world's most pressing challenges.

- **The Dalai Lama, His Holiness.** Tenzin Gyatso, known as the Dalai Lama, is the spiritual leader of Tibet and leads the world in raising awareness of human rights. He became the first Nobel Laureate to be recognized for his concern for global environmental problems.

- **Pope Francis.** The current pope of the Roman Catholic Church is known for his concern for the poor and sense of economic justice. He is the first Jesuit pope and the first pope from the Americas.

- **Bill and Melinda Gates.** Bill Gates, the chairman of Microsoft, and his wife established the Bill & Melinda Gates Foundation, which supports education, global health, and global development.
- **Nelson Mandela.** Nelson Mandela is known worldwide as a symbol of human rights. He fought for the end of apartheid, or racial segregation, in South Africa. After surviving twenty-seven years in prison, he became South Africa's first black president.

activism The practice of supporting one side of a controversial issue.

ambassador A high-ranking person who represents his or her country while living in another country.

amendment A change in the words or meaning of a law or document.

assassinate To murder by sudden or secret attack, often for political reasons.

constitution A system of beliefs and laws that govern a country.

democracy A form of government in which people choose their leader by voting.

diplomat A person who represents his or her country's government while in a foreign country.

human rights Rights, such as freedom from unlawful imprisonment, torture, and execution, that are regarded as belonging fundamentally to all people.

junta A military group controlling a government after taking control of it by force.

parliament A group of people who are responsible for making laws in some kinds of government.

Southeast Asia A region of Asia that refers to countries located south of China.

BOOKS

Aung San Suu Kyi. *Letters from Burma*. New York, NY: Penguin Books, 2010.

Aung San Suu Kyi and Alan Clements. *Voice of Hope: Conversations with Alan Clements*. New York, NY: Seven Stories Press, 2007.

Bengtsson, Jesper. *Aung San Suu Kyi: A Biography*. Lincoln, NE: Potomac Books, 2012.

Popham, Peter. *The Lady and the Peacock: The Life of Aung San Suu Kyi*. New York, NY: The Experiment Publishing, 2012.

Wintle, Justin. *Perfect Hostage: A Life of Aung San Suu Kyi, Burma's Prisoner of Conscience*. New York, NY: Skyhorse Publishing, 2008.

WEBSITES

Because of the changing nature of Internet links, Rosen Publishing has developed an online list of websites related to the subject of this book. This site is updated regularly. Please use this link to access the list:

http://www.rosenlinks.com/mad/aung